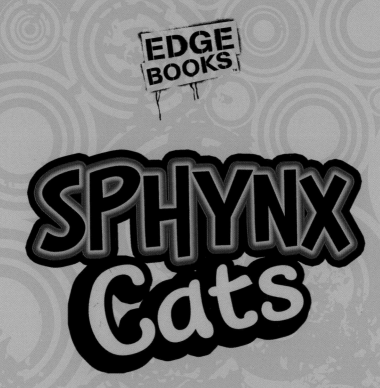

SPHYNX Cats

by Joanne Mattern

CAPSTONE PRESS
a capstone imprint

Edge Books are published by Capstone Press,
151 Good Counsel Drive, P.O. Box 669, Mankato, Minnesota 56002.
www.capstonepub.com

Books published by Capstone Press are manufactured with paper
containing at least 10 percent post-consumer waste.

Library of Congress Cataloging-in-Publication Data
Mattern, Joanne, 1963–
  Sphynx cats / by Joanne Mattern.
    p. cm.—(Edge books. All about cats)
Includes bibliographical references and index.
Summary: "Describes the history, physical features, temperament,
    and care of the Sphynx cat breed"—Provided by publisher.
  ISBN 978-1-4296-6636-7 (library binding)
  1. Sphynx cat—Juvenile literature. I. Title.
  SF449.S68M372 2011
  636.8—dc22   2010041478

Editorial Credits
Connie R. Colwell and Anthony Wacholtz, editors; Heidi Thompson, designer;
    Wanda Winch, media researcher; Eric Manske, production specialist

Photo Credits
iStockphoto: Jacqueline Hunkele, 16, Ruth Ann Johnston, 6; Newscom: AFP/
Timothy A. Clary, 18; Photo by Fiona Green, 5, 21, 22, 24, 26, 29; Shutterstock:
Denis Tabler, 11, Eric Isselée, cover, Kert, 13, Ramzi Hachicho, 9, Vladimir
Kirienko, 15, 19, Zdorov Klrill Vladimirovich, 12

Printed in the United States of America in Stevens Point, Wisconsin.
092010   005934WZS11

TABLE OF CONTENTS

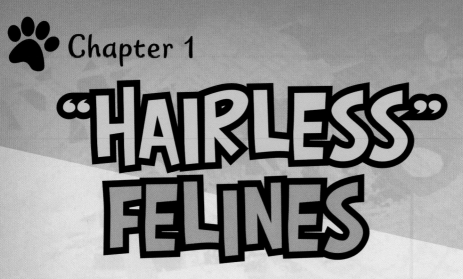

Chapter 1

"HAIRLESS" FELINES

Sphynx cats are one of the easiest cat **breeds** to spot because they have little hair on their bodies. Because of their lack of fur, the cats' other features stand out even more. They have wrinkled skin, large paws, and long toes. The cats also have large ears and wide, oval-shaped eyes.

Sphynx have muscular bodies and are active. But that doesn't mean they don't enjoy cuddling as well. They like to be around people, and they get along with other animals. They love attention and are happy playing with toys or curling up to their owners.

In 2009 the Sphynx was the seventh most popular breed in the Cat Fanciers' Association (CFA). The CFA is the world's largest cat **registry**.

breed—a certain kind of animal within an animal group; breed also means to mate and raise a certain kind of animal

registry—an organization that keeps track of the ancestry for cats of a certain breed

Sphynx are best known for their nearly hairless bodies.

Because the Sphynx breed is rare, you may be put on a waiting list before you can get one.

IS A SPHYNX RIGHT FOR YOU?

People often believe that Sphynx cats make good pets for people who are **allergic** to cats. Some people who are allergic to cat hair can have a Sphynx as a pet. But Sphynx cats' skin still produces flakes called dander. People who are allergic to cat dander may still have an allergic reaction to Sphynx cats. If you are allergic to cats, you should spend some time around a Sphynx before getting one as a pet.

Many people visit animal shelters, breed rescue organizations, or pet stores when they are looking for cats to buy. However, Sphynx cats are rare. Most animal shelters, breed rescue organizations, and pet stores do not have Sphynx available.

If you are interested in adopting a Sphynx, you should contact a breeder. Breeders carefully breed their cats to make sure they are healthy. If you buy a kitten from a breeder, there's a good chance you can meet the kitten's parents. This will give you an idea of how the kitten will look and behave when it grows up.

allergic—having a reaction to certain things such as pollen, dust, or animals

Chapter 2

SPHYNX HISTORY

The Sphynx is one of the world's newest cat breeds. It was first recognized by cat registries in the 1960s. However, hairless cats have been around for a long time. Records of these cats began in the early 1900s. Around 1900 two hairless cats were born in New Mexico. The owners did not breed these cats because they were brother and sister. The cats were called New Mexican Hairless cats. Although they were similar in appearance to today's Sphynx, the two breeds are not related.

The Sphynx cat breed began by accident in 1966. A black and white pet cat in Ontario, Canada, gave birth to a hairless kitten. The owner named the kitten Prune because of its hairless, wrinkled skin. Prune's owner bred him to try to create more hairless kittens. Some of the resulting kittens had hair, while others were hairless. Some people called these kittens Canadian Hairless cats. Others called them Sphynx cats because they looked like an ancient Egyptian statue called the Great Sphinx.

The Great Sphinx in Egypt is at least 4,500 years old.

The early hairless kittens had serious health problems. They did not develop proper immune systems. Cats' immune systems help protect them from diseases. Without immune systems, the cats were more likely to get sick or die. It was not safe to breed these cats because of the health risks. For a time, it looked like the breed would not continue.

In 1975 a cat in Minnesota produced several hairless kittens. One of the kittens, Epidermis, was bred to other cats to create a new line of hairless kittens. The new line helped establish the Sphynx breed in the United States. Epidermis became one of the most important cats in Sphynx history.

In 1978 three hairless kittens were found on the streets in Toronto, Canada. One kitten was male and two were female. The male kitten was named Bambi. The females were named Punkie and Paloma. Bambi stayed in Canada, but the two females were sent to a cat breeder in the Netherlands.

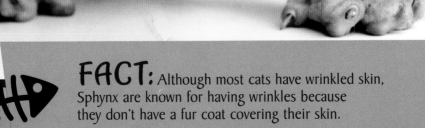

FACT: Although most cats have wrinkled skin, Sphynx are known for having wrinkles because they don't have a fur coat covering their skin.

Devon Rex cats (shown) were bred to hairless cats to create the Sphynx breed.

The breeder used Punkie and Paloma to begin a line of European Sphynx cats. The breeder mated the two females with a male Devon Rex, another cat breed with little body hair. Some offspring of these European Sphynx cats live in North America today.

RECOGNIZING THE BREED

The Sphynx breed had a tough time gaining recognition in the 1970s. Until about 1990, only The International Cat Association (TICA) recognized the Sphynx. The cats could only appear at TICA shows.

Later other cat associations realized the Sphynx was becoming more popular. The associations wanted to include them in their shows as well. In 1998 the CFA recognized the Sphynx.

In 2002 the CFA accepted Sphynx in the main competitive classes at cat shows.

Chapter 3

NO FUR, NO PROBLEM

Today's Sphynx cats are free of the immune system problems of early hairless cats. They are considered a healthy breed. With proper care, Sphynx can live up to 15 years.

Sphynx are medium-sized cats. Most males weigh between 8 and 10 pounds (3.6 and 4.5 kilograms). Females are smaller. Most females weigh between 6 and 8 pounds (2.7 and 3.6 kg).

Sphynx bodies' fit with their playful and energetic nature. They have a sturdy frame, and their bodies are lean and muscular. They have strong tails that are long and tapered.

ALMOST HAIRLESS

Sphynx cats are also called hairless cats, but they do have hair. Very short, fine hair called down covers the cats' bodies. The down may be slightly longer on the cats' ears, nose, tail, and paws. The down makes the Sphynx's body feel like a piece of suede or a warm peach.

tapered—to become narrow at one end
suede—soft leather with a velvet-like surface

The color of a Sphynx is determined by its skin.

A Sphynx's lack of body hair is the result of **genes**. Kittens receive some genes from the mother and some from the father. Genes give cats their eye color, body size, and gender.

Sphynx cats receive two genes that cause them to be hairless. They are called recessive genes and are weaker than other genes. Cats with furry coats sometimes carry one recessive gene for hairlessness. But they have another gene that gives them hair. Cats must receive a recessive hairless gene from each parent to be hairless.

Sphynx kittens receive their hairless genes from both parents.

COLORS

Even though Sphynx cats are basically hairless, their skin can be many different colors. Some of these colors and color patterns include white, black, red, brown, calico, and tortoiseshell. Calico cats are white with patches of black and red. Tortoiseshell cats are a mixture of black and red with few or no white markings.

FACIAL FEATURES

Sphynx cats have unique faces. They have a pointed face that is shaped like a wedge or an upside-down triangle. Because they have no fur, their faces look very narrow. Sphynx cats have long, wide ears and large, oval-shaped eyes.

Cats' whiskers are considered hairs. Sphynx do not have long, straight whiskers like most other cats do. Instead, the whiskers of a Sphynx are short and curly. Many do not have any whiskers at all.

gene—the part of a cell that carries information about how a living thing will look and behave

The eyes of a Sphynx look especially big because of its lack of fur.

PERSONALITY

Sphynx are friendly, intelligent cats. They are affectionate and enjoy being around children and animals. They seem to enjoy being the center of attention. If a Sphynx wants your attention, don't be surprised if it jumps into your lap or weaves between your legs.

If you're looking for a family pet, a Sphynx is a good choice. Sphynx seem to prefer homes with other pets to keep them company. Owners who are often away from the house should consider buying two cats.

Sphynx cats are playful and energetic. They may tear up furniture or curtains if they become bored. Give your Sphynx cat toys or a cat tree to keep it busy.

Sphynx love to play with a variety of cat toys and enjoy swatting at dangling objects.

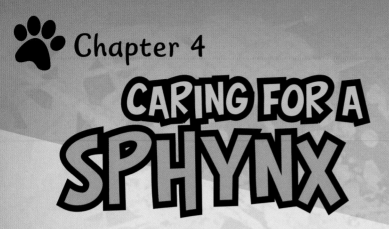

Chapter 4

CARING FOR A SPHYNX

Like other cats, Sphynx should be kept indoors. Cats that roam outdoors are at a much greater risk of developing diseases than indoor cats. Outdoor cats also face dangers from cars and other animals.

Outdoor Sphynx cats face other dangers as well. Because Sphynx have little hair, they have a hard time staying warm. The lack of fur also puts them at risk of being overexposed to the sun's rays. Without any fur, their skin could burn. Sphynx cats should be kept inside where the temperature is comfortable for them.

FEEDING

Sphynx need nutritious cat food. They have fast **metabolisms**. Many cat foods in supermarkets or pet stores provide a balanced, healthy diet for Sphynx cats.

metabolism—the rate at which food changes into energy

Making sure your cat gets a lot of attention is an important part of its care.

One option is to feed your cat dry food. Dry food is less expensive than other types of food. It will not spoil if left out in a dish. Another option is to feed your cat moist, canned food. Canned food will spoil if it is left out for more than one hour. If you decide to give your cat moist food, you should feed twice each day for adult cats. The amount of food needed depends on the individual cat. You can ask a veterinarian for advice on which type of cat food is best.

Dry cat food comes in small pieces so cats can easily chew and swallow it.

Cats need to drink water to stay healthy. They should always have fresh, clean water available. Be sure to replace the water in the bowls each day.

LITTER BOXES

Cats also need to have a litter box. Most litter is made of clay, but it can also be made out of wood, wheat, or corn. When you fill the litter box, the litter should be 2 to 3 inches (5 to 7.6 centimeters) deep. Remember to clean the waste out of the box each day. You should also change the litter often, preferably at least once every two weeks. Your Sphynx may refuse to use a dirty litter box.

litter—small bits of clay or other material used to absorb the waste of cats and other animals

GROOMING

Sphynx have little hair, but they still need to be groomed. Cats' coats often absorb the oils from their skin, but Sphynx coats can't do this job. Sphynx must be bathed about once every one to two weeks to keep their skin free of oils. Most pet stores sell special shampoo made for cats. The hard part will be getting your Sphynx in the tub.

Most cats don't like baths, but they usually enjoy being wrapped in a towel afterward.

Cats usually do not like to be bathed. It is important to start bathing your Sphynx when it is a kitten. The kitten will then become used to taking baths. You should also rub your Sphynx with a damp, soft cloth every day to absorb body oil.

The Sphynx's ears require special care. The hair inside cats' ears usually helps keep out dirt and wax. But Sphynx's ears are hairless and very large. The insides of their ears often get dirty. Owners should wipe out their cats' ears with a soft, wet washcloth or a damp cotton ball every week.

DENTAL CARE

Sphynx need regular dental care to protect their teeth and gums from plaque. Plaque can cause tooth decay and gum disease.

You should brush your cats' teeth at least once each week. You can use a toothbrush made for cats or a soft cloth. Be sure to use toothpaste made for cats. Your cat may become sick if it swallows toothpaste made for people.

Brushing alone may not be enough to remove the plaque from older cats' teeth. They may need to have their teeth cleaned once each year by a veterinarian.

plaque—a coating of germs and saliva on teeth that can cause tooth decay

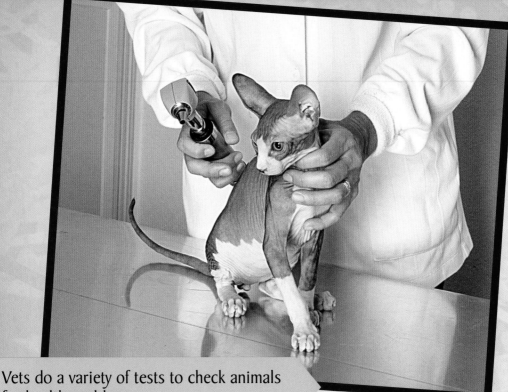

Vets do a variety of tests to check animals for health problems.

NAIL CARE

Sphynx cats need their nails trimmed every few weeks. Trimming helps reduce damage if cats scratch on the carpet or furniture. It also protects cats from infections caused by ingrown nails. An ingrown nail occurs when the nail grows into the bottom of the cat's paw.

You should use a special nail clipper when trimming your cat's nails. A veterinarian can show you the proper way to trim nails. It is best to begin trimming a cat's nails when it is a kitten. The kitten will get used to having its nails trimmed as it grows older.

FACT: Many vets suggest clipping the nails of a Sphynx after a bath. You should wrap the cat in a warm blanket to dry it off and expose one paw at a time as you begin to cut.

SCRATCHING POSTS

Cats mark their territories by leaving their scent on objects they scratch. Cats also scratch to release tension and keep their claws sharp. This habit can be a problem if cats scratch furniture, carpet, or curtains.

To keep your Sphynx from destroying the furniture, provide it with a scratching post from a pet store. You could also make one from wood and rope. Scratching posts at least 3 feet (.9 m) tall work best.

HEALTH CARE

Sphynx cats no longer have problems with their immune systems like early Sphynx. But they can still become sick or **inherit** diseases like other cats.

Responsible cat breeders test their animals for inherited diseases. They do not breed animals that suffer from serious illnesses. Breeders should have information on their cats' medical histories. If you buy your Sphynx from a breeder, you should review the cat's medical history. If you are planning to buy a kitten, it would be helpful to view its parents' medical histories.

inherit—to receive a characteristic from a parent

Sphynx cats must visit a vet regularly for checkups. Most vets recommend yearly visits for cats. Older cats usually have more health problems than younger cats. They may need to visit the vet two or three times each year. You should take your Sphynx to the vet for a checkup soon after you get it. The vet will check the cat's heart, lungs, eyes, ears, and mouth.

The vet will also give your Sphynx **vaccinations** to prevent serious diseases. Serious cat diseases include rabies and feline leukemia. Rabies is a deadly disease that is spread by animal bites. Feline leukemia attacks a cat's immune system. The disease spreads from cat to cat by bodily fluids.

Veterinarians also spay female cats and neuter male cats. These surgeries make it impossible for cats to have kittens, which helps control the pet population. The surgeries help prevent diseases such as infections and some types of cancer. Spayed and neutered cats also usually have calmer personalities than cats that don't get the surgery. Owners who aren't planning to breed their cats should have them spayed or neutered.

The Sphynx's unique look, playful nature, and loving attitude make it a great choice for a family pet. People who own a Sphynx appreciate it as an intelligent, friendly companion.

vaccination—a shot of medicine that protects animals from a disease

With love, care, and attention, your Sphynx can make a great companion for many years.

GLOSSARY

allergic (a-LUHR-jik)—having a reaction to certain things such as pollen, dust, or animals

breed (BREED)—a certain kind of animal within an animal group; breed also means to mate and raise a certain kind of animal

gene (JEEN)—the part of a cell that carries information about how a living thing will look and behave

inherit (in-HAIR-it)—to receive a characteristic from a parent

litter (LIT-ur)—small bits of clay or other material used to absorb the waste of cats and other animals

metabolism (muh-TAB-uh-liz-uhm)—the rate at which food changes into energy

plaque (PLAK)—the coating of food, saliva, and bacteria that forms on teeth and can cause tooth decay

registry (REH-juh-stree)—an organization that keeps track of the ancestry for cats of a certain breed

suede (SWAYD)—soft leather with a velvet-like surface

taper (TAY-pur)—to become more narrow on one end

vaccination (vak-suh-NAY-shun)—a shot of medicine that protects animals from a disease

READ MORE

Furstinger, Nancy. *Sphynx Cats*. Checkerboard Animal Library. Edina, Minn.: ABDO Publishing, 2006.

Landau, Elaine. *Sphynx Are the Best!* The Best Cats Ever. Minneapolis: Lerner, 2011.

Rau, Dana Meachen. *Top 10 Cats for Kids*. Top Pets for Kids With American Humane. Berkeley Heights, N.J.: Enslow Elementary, 2009.

INTERNET SITES

FactHound offers a safe, fun way to find Internet sites related to this book. All of the sites on FactHound have been researched by our staff.

Here's all you do:

Visit *www.facthound.com*

Type in this code: 9781429666367

Super-cool stuff!

Check out projects, games and lots more at
www.capstonekids.com

INDEX